Long ago, in the land of Israel, there
was a priest called Eli. He served God
in the temple. When he was a young
man he loved God very much.

By the time he was an old man he had two sons. They did not care about God. They were cruel and greedy and the Israelites were afraid of them.

God speaks
to Samuel

Story by Penny Frank
Illustrated by Tony Morris

THE LION
STORY BIBLE

16

TRING · BELLEVILLE · SYDNEY

The Bible tells us how God chose the Israelites to be his special people. He made them a promise that he would always love and care for them. But they must obey him.

This story tells how God especially chose a little boy to serve him. You can find this story in your own Bible, in the first book of Samuel chapters 1 to 3.

Copyright © 1985 Lion Publishing
Published by
Lion Publishing plc
Icknield Way, Tring, Herts, England
ISBN 0 85648 741 4
Lion Publishing Corporation
10885 Textile Road, Belleville,
Michigan 48111, USA
ISBN 0 85648 741 4
Albatross Books Pty Ltd
PO Box 320, Sutherland, NSW 2232, Australia
ISBN 0 86760 525 1

First edition 1985
Reprinted 1986

Printed and bound in Hong Kong

British Library Cataloguing in Publication Data

Frank, Penny
God speaks to Samuel. – (The Lion Story Bible; 16)
1. Samuel – Juvenile literature
I. Title
222'.40924   BS580.S2

ISBN 0-85648-741-4

Library of Congress Cataloging in Publication Data

Frank, Penny.
God speaks to Samuel.
(The Lion Story Bible; 16)
1. Samuel (Biblical judge)—Juvenile literature. 2. Bible. O.T.—Biography—Juvenile literature. [1. Samuel (Biblical judge) 2. Bible stories—O.T.] I. Morris, Tony, ill. II. Title. III. Series: Frank, Penny. Lion Story Bible; 16.
BS580.S2F68 1985   222'.4309505
84-25021
ISBN 0-85648-741-4

The Israelites wanted a priest who
really loved God and would show them
the right way to live.

One of the Israelite women was called
Hannah. She was very sad, because she
had no children. She had often asked
God to give her a baby.

The worst times were when Hannah and her husband met all their friends for a feast at the temple in Shiloh.

'Haven't you had a baby yet?' they would ask. Hannah just shook her head and looked sad.

One time Hannah left the feast.
She was crying and she could not eat.
She went into God's house, where it was
quiet.

Eli, the old priest, was sitting in
his place by the door. But she did not

want to talk to Eli. She wanted to talk
to God.

Hannah stood there, praying. Her lips
moved but she made no sound.
    'Dear God, please give me a son,'
she begged. 'I promise he will serve
you all his life, here in your temple.
You can see how unhappy I am.'

Eli came up to Hannah. He did not
know she was praying.

'What's the matter with you?' he said.
'Have you had too much wine at the
feast?'

'Oh no!' said Hannah, and she told him
why she was talking to God.

    'I'm sure God will hear you,' said
Eli.

    Hannah felt much better as she went
back to the feast.

They went back home and very soon Hannah had some good news for her husband.

'God heard me,' she told him. 'I'm going to have a baby at last.'

When the baby was born, he was
beautiful. His hair was curly and his
hands were so tiny.

Hannah said he was the best baby
boy who had ever been born. They
called him Samuel.

Later on, Hannah had more children.
When Samuel was old enough,
Hannah took him to the temple, just as
she had promised. She missed him very
much but she was glad she had someone
so special to give to God.

She knew that Eli was very kind. She
wanted Samuel to grow up to love and
serve God.

Every year, when Hannah came to the
feast, she brought Samuel new clothes
she had made for him.

For a long time God had not been able
to talk to Eli. Eli was too busy
thinking about his wicked sons,
who did not care about God.
  In those days only a few people
listened to what God had to say.

God wanted to talk to Samuel. He knew
that Samuel had never heard his voice.
   'I will speak to him at bedtime,
when it is quiet,' God said.

One night, Samuel was sleeping in the temple.

'Samuel,' said a voice.

'Here I am,' replied Samuel, thinking it was Eli. He went over to the old priest. But Eli had not called him. 'Go back to bed,' said Eli.

Then Samuel heard the voice again.

 He got up and went to Eli. But Eli had not called him. So he went back to bed.

'Samuel,' said the voice for the third
time.

Samuel got up and went to Eli once
again.

Then Eli said, 'God must be speaking
to you. Listen carefully to what he says.
Now go back to bed.'

When Samuel heard the voice again, he answered as Eli had told him. 'Speak, Lord, I am listening.'

God had a special message for him to give to Eli.

'Tell Eli that his sons have been very wicked,' God said. 'He has not made them stop, and I am going to punish them.'

Samuel did not want to make Eli sad, but he knew he must give him the message.

Eli knew that what God had said was true.

After that Samuel often heard God
talking to him. Because he did as God
said, the people could trust him.
He showed them the right way to live.

The Lion Story Bible is made up of 52 individual stories for young readers, building up an understanding of the Bible as one story — God's story — a story for all time and all people.

The Old Testament section (numbers 1–30) tells the story of a great nation — God's chosen people, the Israelites — and God's love and care for them through good times and bad. The stories are about people who knew and trusted God. From this nation came one special person, Jesus Christ, sent by God to save all people everywhere.

God speaks to Samuel comes from the first of the two Old Testament books which bear Samuel's name, chapters 1 to 3. God's people, settled in the land he gave them, had suffered a number of invasions because they were disloyal to him. In answer to their cries for help he sent a series of champions, the Judges, to lead them and set them free. The birth of Samuel marks the end of this time. Before long Israel will have a king, chosen by Samuel under God's direction. Set apart to serve God from birth, Samuel remained God's faithful servant all his life long.

The next book in the series, number 17: *A king for Israel*, takes up the story of Samuel the king-maker.